LEARN MEDIA LITERACY SKILLS

HOW TO IDENTIFY
FALSE INFORMATION

by Tom Streissguth

BrightPoint Press

San Diego, CA

© 2025 BrightPoint Press
an imprint of ReferencePoint Press, Inc.
Printed in the United States

For more information, contact:
BrightPoint Press
PO Box 27779
San Diego, CA 92198
www.BrightPointPress.com

ALL RIGHTS RESERVED.

No part of this work covered by the copyright hereon may be reproduced or used in any form or by any means—graphic, electronic, or mechanical, including photocopying, recording, taping, web distribution, or information storage retrieval systems—without the written permission of the publisher.

LIBRARY OF CONGRESS CATALOGING-IN-PUBLICATION DATA

Name: Streissguth, Tom, author.
Title: How to identify false information / by Tom Streissguth.
Description: San Diego, CA: BrightPoint Press, 2025 | Series: Learn media literacy skills | Audience: Grade 7 to 9 | Includes bibliographical references and index.
Identifiers: ISBN: 9781678209728 (hardcover) | ISBN: 9781678209735 (eBook)
The complete Library of Congress record is available at www.loc.gov.

CONTENTS

AT A GLANCE	**4**
INTRODUCTION NOTHING BUT A HOAX	**6**
CHAPTER ONE FAKE NEWS AND CONSPIRACY THEORIES	**12**
CHAPTER TWO PROPAGANDA	**24**
CHAPTER THREE CLICKBAIT AND FAKE PHOTOS	**36**
CHAPTER FOUR SPOTTING FALSE INFORMATION	**48**
Glossary	**58**
Source Notes	**59**
For Further Research	**60**
Index	**62**
Image Credits	**63**
About the Author	**64**

AT A GLANCE

- Today, more information is available to people than ever before. The internet and social media provide an endless stream of information.

- Bias is when something or someone unfairly favors one point of view over another. Bias is common in some areas of news media. Readers can spot bias by reading sources critically and carefully.

- Propaganda is the practice of using bias to support a single point of view. Propaganda relies on deception, false information, and headlines that appeal to emotions such as fear or suspicion.

- A story designed as propaganda may use silly names or descriptors for an opponent. Propagandists may also use negative or positive words to persuade readers to agree with their point of view.

- Many internet stories are written to advertise and sell products. Clickbait headlines are misleading. They convince curious readers to click through to a web page and view stories and ads.

- Images can be doctored. This means that what is shown in a photograph may be false. The technology used to make fake pictures and videos is available to everyone.

- Fact-checking websites can help readers determine whether claims made on the internet or in other forms of media are truthful.

INTRODUCTION

NOTHING BUT A HOAX

In April 1844, readers of the *New York Sun* newspaper saw a headline on the front page. It said "Astounding News! The Atlantic Crossed in Three Days!"[1] The article described a hot-air balloon voyage. The balloon had traveled across the ocean. Mr. Monck Mason piloted the balloon. It took off from England. It landed in Charleston, South Carolina.

Throughout the mid- to late 1800s, the *New York Sun* was known for publishing sensational stories. Its building was in an area of New York City known as Newspaper Row.

The story caught readers' attention. Crowds mobbed the *New York Sun*'s offices. People rushed to buy the paper. Mason's voyage seemed impossible. Everyone wanted to read the story.

Edgar Allan Poe is known for writing mysteries, horror stories, and poetry. He wrote several hoax stories during his lifetime.

For two days, everyone in New York talked about Mason's balloon. But then the newspaper revealed the story was fake. It was just a **hoax**. It was written by a writer named Edgar Allan Poe. He admitted he wrote the fake story. He wanted to see if people would believe it.

TOO MUCH INFORMATION

This true story is an example of fake news. Fake news refers to false news stories. Sometimes people write fake news on purpose. They want to mislead readers. Or they want to influence public opinion.

Fake news can be either misinformation or disinformation. Misinformation is inaccurate or **exaggerated** information. People spread it on accident. They do not

Today, many people read news stories online or watch news coverage on television. The wide range of news sources available can make it difficult for people to know which sources to trust.

mean to deceive others. Disinformation is deliberately false information. It is created to deceive people.

Today, people get information from many sources. They read news online. They listen to stories on television or the radio. Stories from these sources often seem true. But some sources contain false information. A story may have a shocking headline. It may give a false account of an event. Writers might make up facts.

There are many stories in the media. This can make it hard to know whether information is true. But there are ways to identify false information. Using these tools can help readers think critically about what they read. It can help them navigate the world of information.

CHAPTER ONE

FAKE NEWS AND CONSPIRACY THEORIES

Disinformation and misinformation are types of fake news. These types of false information can have many purposes. They can be used to sell products. They may be used to support political campaigns.

Other times, false information is shared for fun. *The Onion* is a website that publishes outrageous stories. The stories are satire. This content makes

People may encounter misinformation and disinformation while browsing the internet or scrolling through social media platforms.

fun of serious people and events. Most people know stories from *The Onion* are false. But some people quote the site's stories as true. They were tricked into believing them. Or they want to trick others.

Social media platforms such as Instagram suggest posts, pages, or ads to users based on content they've liked in the past.

SOCIAL MEDIA AND WEBSITES

Many news headlines appear on social media platforms. Social media sites tailor content to users. They collect information about users. They track the websites users visit. They track products users order. They even know which stories users have liked.

Social media companies use this information. Computer programs decide which news stories to show users. They may try to get users to click on sponsored stories. These look like news stories. But they are really ads for products. Because of this, it is easy for fake news to spread online.

In the past, some news outlets had gatekeepers. These people checked information before it was shared with the public. Today, editors at news agencies continue to fact-check information. If they can't **verify** it, they cut it from the story.

Some websites are run by news organizations. These sites include fact-checked information. But some sites do not. Social media platforms do not always verify information on their sites. Other sites use misleading headlines.

5G Conspiracy

Many conspiracy theories arose in 2020 during the COVID-19 pandemic. On social media, people shared stories about phone towers. They claimed the towers spread the disease. They blamed a cell phone technology called 5G. After hearing this fake news, vandals attacked 5G antenna towers in Great Britain.

CONSPIRACY THEORIES

Conspiracy theories are another type of fake news. A conspiracy theory is an idea or story that someone makes up. It offers an explanation of why or how an event happened. Often, conspiracy theories claim an event occurred because of a plot. They say the plot was planned by powerful people. A conspiracy theory may have some facts right. But it gets others wrong.

In 1969, humans landed on the moon for the first time. Astronauts collected moon rocks. They planted the US flag in the soil. Millions of people watched the landing on television.

For some people, the moon landing seems unbelievable. They think the landing was faked. They claim that astronauts acted

The astronauts who landed on the moon in 1969 took photos during their mission. One photo shows Buzz Aldrin walking on the moon's surface. Some people believe these photos are fake.

on a stage. They give facts that they believe support this conspiracy theory. Some say that with no air on the moon, the US flag shouldn't look like it is waving. However, the truth is that the flag had a horizontal support along the top. When astronauts twisted the flag into the soil, the flag appeared to wave.

People have created conspiracy theories to explain many events. One is President John F. Kennedy's murder in 1963. Some people believe government agencies or gangs arranged the murder.

Another conspiracy theory is about the COVID-19 pandemic. The pandemic began in the United States in 2020. Some theorists claimed people created the COVID-19 virus in a lab. Other theories are about COVID-19 vaccines. Some believe these vaccines are dangerous. There is no evidence for any of these theories.

BE SKEPTICAL

While **evaluating** a story, readers must be aware of their opinions. A writer might express opinions about an election. A reader might share these opinions. This can make him more willing to believe the story. This is called confirmation bias. It means people are more likely to believe information that supports their opinions.

Social media sites often rely on confirmation bias. If readers agree with a writer's opinion, they'll likely believe the story. They may do so even if the story is false. Readers may also be more likely to share the story. This can make more people visit the web page. As a result, the site makes more money through ads.

During the COVID-19 pandemic, conspiracy theories about the virus led some people to protest vaccine and mask requirements.

Because of this, readers should be skeptical of what they read online. They should look for evidence that the information is accurate. They should check

21

At many schools, colleges, and libraries, students can learn how to evaluate sources and identify false information.

its sources. Readers shouldn't believe things without supporting evidence.

Annie Zeidman-Karpinski is a librarian. She works at the University of Oregon. She recommends using the SIFT method to evaluate information. SIFT stands for Stop, Investigate, Find, and Trace.

First, the reader should stop when she encounters information. Then she should investigate the information's sources. Next, she should find better coverage of the information. Finally, she should identify any quotes or data in the content. She should trace these back to their sources. Zeidman-Karpinski said, "SIFT is just an acronym you can do in any order. . . . Think about where everything is coming from and decide what you are going to do."[2]

CHAPTER TWO

PROPAGANDA

Some false stories are used as propaganda. This is information used to change people's minds about a topic. It presents information in a **deceptive** way. Propaganda may be used to convince people to believe something. It may try to persuade people to support one side of an issue. It has long been a political tool. Some governments use propaganda. They may use it to gain support for a war effort.

The character of Uncle Sam was often used on posters to encourage Americans to join the army during World War I.

Companies might use propaganda in ads. They might try to persuade people to buy a product.

Propaganda deceives readers by using certain words. Some words make people feel scared. Others create positive feelings. Propaganda may also leave out or exaggerate information. Other times, it lies. It can be found in all forms of media.

PROPAGANDA METHODS

There are many propaganda techniques. In 1939, Alfred and Elizabeth Lee published a book about this. It was called *The Fine Art of Propaganda*. In the book, the Lees defined seven common propaganda tools.

One is name-calling. Silly or strange names are used in propaganda. These

Former US president Donald Trump has used propaganda methods such as name-calling. During his 2020 presidential campaign, Trump used social media to spread this kind of messaging.

names can ridicule someone. A name can also make audiences fearful. For example, a **conservative** politician may be called "extreme." A **liberal** candidate might be labeled a "radical." Propagandists may call political opponents "corrupt" or "crooked."

Another propaganda tool is known as the glittering **generality**. Propagandists often

27

use words or phrases that sound positive or negative. But these words carry little real meaning. When describing food products, a propagandist might use the words "natural" and "green." These words make the product seem healthier.

Transfer is another propaganda method. It involves connecting an idea with positive images. The US flag is often used in this

Bots and Trolls

Bots and trolls can be useful for propagandists. Bots are computer programs that can imitate humans. They are used to push stories to social media users. A shocking headline on a person's Facebook feed may come from a bot. A troll is someone who wants to get a strong reaction online. Trolls spread false information to many people. They often do so on websites or social media.

way. Politicians may appear in ads with the US flag in the background. This is meant to make them look patriotic.

Some propaganda relies on testimonials. This might involve a famous person endorsing something. A movie star might claim to use a product. If a product is approved by someone popular, people might want to buy it. This is a common advertising tool. Professional athletes often do endorsements for brands. They are paid to say they use the product.

Another type of propaganda is the "plain folks" method. This is a common **tactic** in political campaigns. Candidates are filmed inside local restaurants or stores. The politicians talk with ordinary people there. This makes candidates seem like they understand voters. The candidate promises to work on the customers' behalf if they elect him. Later, the customers express good opinions of the candidate. This is a way to gain support among TV audiences. But the people in the video are often actors.

Card stacking is also a propaganda tool. It means listing all the positive things about something. One example is a celebrity's fan website. The site might list all the hit movies the star has appeared in. But it leaves out the celebrity's failed projects.

Propagandists may use the bandwagon method, too. These messages may describe a growing number of people buying a product. Others are urged to join the movement. People may feel pressured to follow the trend.

Some propaganda tactics, such as testimonials or the bandwagon method, can persuade people to buy products online.

GOVERNMENT PROPAGANDA

Sometimes governments use propaganda. This is an issue in North Korea. This small country is in eastern Asia. It is under a dictatorship. This means one group has absolute rule over the country. The dictatorship controls the media that people see. It limits freedom of speech. North Korea's government surrounds people with propaganda. It does this to influence their ideas about the country.

Posters are one type of North Korean propaganda. One poster shows a housewife surrounded by appliances. The poster says, "Let's Build Small and Medium

Many North Korean propaganda posters feature brightly colored images and slogans about the country's progress.

Sized Power Plants and Send More Electricity to Factories and Villages!"[3] Power outages happen frequently in North Korea. Fewer than half of the country's households have electricity. But the poster tells people the country is making progress. It urges people to help.

When a government controls all information, propaganda can be easy to spread. In North Korea, the internet is not available to most people. The government publishes all newspapers.

But propaganda can also thrive in places where lots of information is available. In the United States, there are few limits on the media. Writers can exaggerate and lie. This makes it easy to spread propaganda.

The popular character Captain America has appeared in many movies and TV shows. But the superhero started out as a 1940s propaganda figure.

One example of US propaganda is the hero Captain America. Captain America comic books first appeared in March 1941. This was just before the United States entered World War II (1939–1945). Captain America embodied American values such as freedom. He fought villains that looked like real-life war enemies. The books were designed to increase support for the US war effort.

KERNEL OF TRUTH

The secret of propaganda is that it relies on a little bit of truth. Richard Stengel wrote the book *Information Wars.* In the book, he wrote, "The most effective forms of disinformation are a mixture of information that is both true and false."[4] For example, a writer can use a real statistic to express a false idea. A quote can be used out of context. It might be part of a longer quote.

These kernels of truth can convince people to believe propaganda. That's why it's important to read different sources. By getting information from more than one place, readers can learn the truth.

CHAPTER THREE

CLICKBAIT AND FAKE PHOTOS

Sometimes internet users encounter false information through clickbait. Clickbait is a story written to get people to click on it. The more visitors the site gets, the more money it earns from ads.

Clickbait headlines often try to tempt or interest readers. They may seem fantastic or weird. The more outrageous the headline, the more people it will attract. The headline "Puppy Swims

People may encounter strange, confusing, or unbelievable headlines on the internet. These types of headlines are likely clickbait.

the Stormy Atlantic!" might appear on a Facebook news feed. A user might think the headline sounds unbelievable. But some

In 2018, Facebook created ads that warned users about clickbait on the platform.

dogs are good swimmers. Many Facebook users like posts about puppies. The user might be curious.

When she clicks the headline, the web browser jumps to a new page. The story appears. The real story turns out to be about a puppy on a cruise ship. It sailed across the ocean with the passengers. It loved to swim in the pool. The Facebook user was fooled by the clickbait headline. It made her believe something that wasn't true.

Fake news headlines are used to mislead readers. The headlines may repeat a story's false information. They may include inaccurate details. Readers should be skeptical about strange headlines.

USING EMOTIONS

Clickbait writers want readers to engage with their stories. The writers want people to click on the headlines. They want them to look at the pictures. They also want readers to see ads. Ads appear by the article. Attracting people to the article means more people will see the ads. They might buy things. That's how the site earns money.

Clickbait writers often use emotions, too. Some clickbait headlines use fear words. Examples of these include "scary" and "horrible." Outrage is another key emotion. If people get upset about something, they are more likely to share a story. Jonah Berger is a professor. He works at the University of Pennsylvania. He said, "Anger, anxiety, humor, excitement, inspiration, surprise—all of these are punchy emotions that clickbait headlines rely on."[5] Upset readers are more likely to believe information. That's why readers must stay calm and be aware of what they're reading.

FAKE IMAGES

Images can also spread false information. Sometimes this can cause confusion. March 10, 2024, was Mother's Day in the United Kingdom. A photo appeared

Big Consequences

In 2013, hackers took over the Associated Press's Twitter account. The hackers used the account to spread fake news. They announced that bombs had exploded at the White House. This fake news caused the stock market to crash. The market lost about $136 billion in value.

online and in print. The photo showed Kate Middleton. She is the Princess of Wales. She was posing with her three children. Everyone was smiling. The picture showed that all was well with the royal family.

Kate Middleton (in white) attended a royal event in June 2024. Earlier that year she shared an altered photo of her family. This caused confusion and rumors.

Press agencies included the photo in their reports. For a few hours, the photo remained online. But then it disappeared.

The photo came from Kensington Palace. This is a historic home for the British royal family. The palace has a press office. It provides information and photos related to the family. It works with independent agencies. These supply news to media outlets.

But independent press agencies work to share accurate information. Their reputation depends on the careful screening of information. The Associated Press (AP) is a leading press agency. AP editors looked closely at Middleton's photo. They noticed some problems. In several spots, the image had been altered. A zipper didn't line up.

One sleeve of a sweater did not match the other. The AP took the photo out of circulation. News agencies removed it from their websites.

The next day, Middleton sent out an apology. She said releasing the photo was a mistake. She posted about it on social media. She wrote, "Like many amateur photographers, I do occasionally experiment with editing. I wanted to express my apologies for any confusion the family photograph we shared yesterday caused."[6]

WHY FAKES?

Some images shared online are the result of editing mistakes. But some people alter images to fool others. They may create a photo of themselves standing by a celebrity.

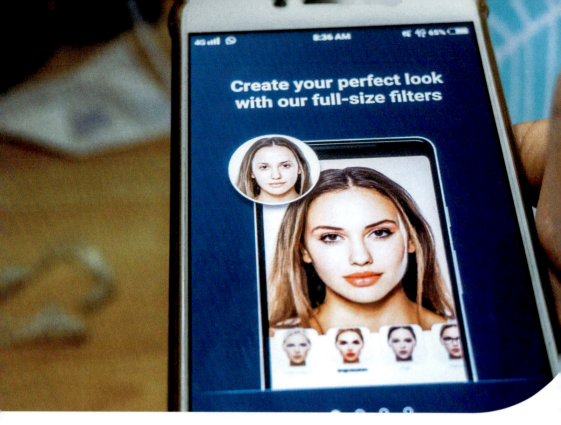

Apps such as FaceApp make it easy for people to create deepfakes. The app allows users to alter the faces or physical features of people in photos.

Other times, people who alter images or videos have political goals. They may create a fake TikTok video of a candidate dancing. This can make the candidate look silly. The video may not fool many people. But it might affect how some people vote.

Fake images are commonly used on fake social media accounts. These accounts use

People can use online resources such as reverse image programs to help identify fake images.

a person's real name and identity. But the account is used to bully the person. A real picture can be altered to make a person look like he's doing something illegal.

Deepfakes are another type of fake image. These are created by combining two real videos or images. Someone's face may be combined with another person's body. A skilled editor can create realistic deepfakes.

REVERSE SEARCHING

People can use tools to detect fake images. One is the reverse image search. This software is available online. It can help users find image sources. The user uploads an image to the tool. The software shows where else the image appears online. This can help people determine whether the image has been used by trustworthy sources. It can also help people locate the original image. They can track how it has been altered.

Google, Yahoo!, and Bing have reverse image search tools. The TinEye site can tell users how an image has been changed. The site also tracks all the places the picture has been used online.

CHAPTER FOUR

SPOTTING FALSE INFORMATION

There are several ways readers can spot false information. First, the reader should fact-check any statistics or dates included in a story. Next, the reader should check the author's name. He can search for other stories written by the author.

The reader should also check any sources mentioned in the story. The story might lack sources and links. This can be a sign of sloppy research. It could also mean

Readers should use reliable sources to verify whether information is true. The Centers for Disease Control and Prevention (CDC) is a reliable source for information about health issues such as COVID-19.

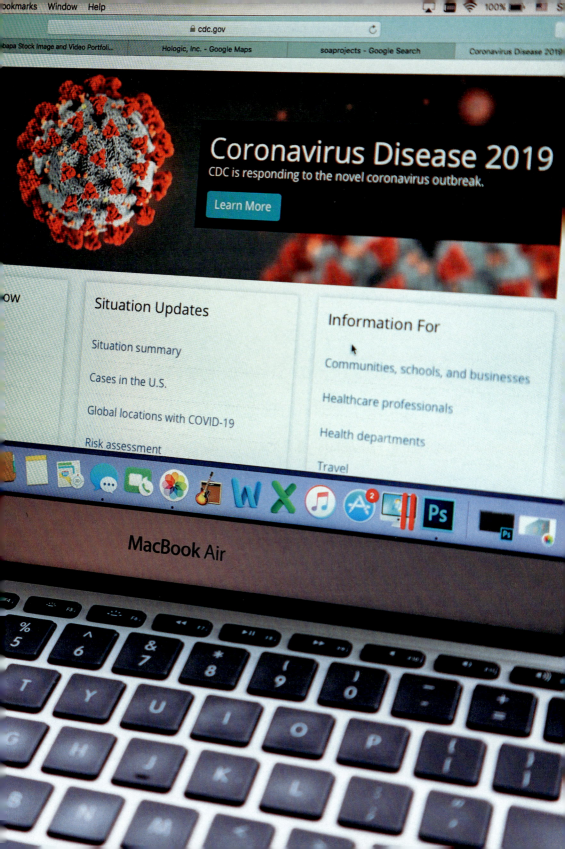

the information is made up. If there are links to sources, the reader should follow them. He should check if the sources are reliable. Some links may take readers to unreliable web pages. This can be a sign that a source is not trustworthy.

Stories without data or reliable sources might be fake news. Sharing the story would spread disinformation. This is why it's important to verify a story before sharing.

Fact-Checking Websites

Fact-checking websites can be a helpful tool. Most are run by editors and reporters. Some fact-checking sites are FactCheck.org and Snopes.com. Many news organizations run their own fact-checking sites. The *Washington Post* has a fact-checking site called Fact Checker.

SPOTTING CONSPIRACY THEORIES

To spot conspiracy theories, readers should use **authoritative** sources. For example, many authors have written books about President Kennedy's murder. Professional medical organizations have reported on COVID-19.

Readers should pay attention to the language used in a source. They should watch for language that creates suspicion and doubt. They should look for language that inspires strong emotions.

People can also use fact-checking websites. The PolitiFact site focuses on politics and current events. FactCheck.org has a SciCheck page. The website says, "FactCheck.org's SciCheck feature focuses

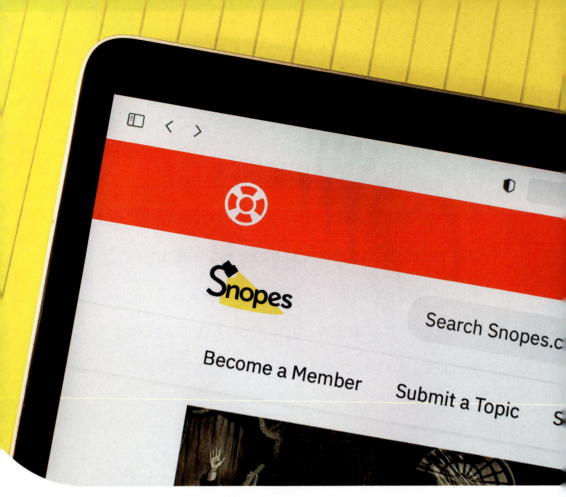

Snopes.com is a fact-checking website that covers a wide range of topics, including politics, current events, and folklore.

exclusively on false and misleading scientific claims that are made by partisans to influence public policy."[7] Readers can bookmark fact-checking sites with their web browser. This makes it easy to access the sites.

SPOTTING DEEPFAKES

To spot deepfakes, internet users can check the source of photos and videos. A credit line should give the source. It should note who took the picture. It should say where the picture first appeared. Users must consider if the source is trustworthy. If no source is given, the picture might be fake.

Next, users should examine the image. A face or head may have been swapped out. The skin color of the face might not match that of other body parts. They should check if the lighting matches the photo's background. There may be unusual shadows, colors, or bright spots.

In videos, people should watch to see if a person's lip movements match the audio.

They should consider whether the person's expression matches what she is saying. What is the subject doing? Does the action seem realistic?

PAY ATTENTION

Xavier Harding writes about misinformation on the internet. "Misleading news content . . . is all around us—in our phones and on our feeds; in our timelines and on our screens," he said. "The easiest way you can limit the spread of fake news is to stop sharing it yourself."[8] To stay informed, readers should learn how to spot false information online.

Readers should learn about a story's author. They should try to understand why the author wrote the story. They can look up

People can research methods for spotting deepfakes. Many college libraries have web pages that provide tips and tricks for spotting fake images and other types of false information.

the author's name to see if she is qualified. Readers should also think about the writer's motives. Is she telling readers something out of the goodness of her heart? Or does she want people to do something for her?

It can also be helpful to check a writer's sources. This is like detective work. Readers should research the experts mentioned in a source. They should find out if they're really experts. Finally, readers should consider if the writer supports her facts with evidence. Does the author rely on opinions instead of facts? If so, readers might be dealing with fake news. Following these strategies can help readers detect false information.

SPOTTING FALSE INFORMATION CHECKLIST

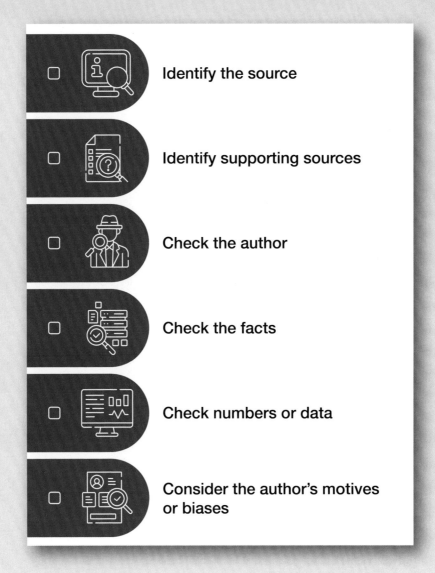

- ☐ Identify the source
- ☐ Identify supporting sources
- ☐ Check the author
- ☐ Check the facts
- ☐ Check numbers or data
- ☐ Consider the author's motives or biases

There are several steps readers can take to identify false information. These include finding supporting sources, researching an article's author, and checking the facts.

GLOSSARY

authoritative
reliable, knowledgeable, and accurate

conservative
describing a viewpoint that favors established customs

deceptive
describing something that misleads others

evaluating
determining something's value, accuracy, or importance

exaggerated
overstated

generality
a vague, nonspecific statement

hoax
an act or prank meant to trick people

liberal
describing a viewpoint that favors social change

tactic
a method for accomplishing something, such as a task

verify
to determine the accuracy or truth of something

SOURCE NOTES

INTRODUCTION: NOTHING BUT A HOAX

1. Quoted in John Tresch, "The Balloon-Hoax of Edgar Allan Poe and Early New York Grifters," *Literary Hub*, June 16, 2021. http://lithub.com.

CHAPTER ONE: FAKE NEWS AND CONSPIRACY THEORIES

2. Quoted in "What Misinformation Looks Like and Tools to Combat It," *Oregon Health News Blog*, December 3, 2021. http://covidblog.oregon.gov.

CHAPTER TWO: PROPAGANDA

3. "Let's Wash Our Hands! North Korea Coronavirus Propaganda Poster," *Koryo Studio*, June 2020. http://koryostudio.com.

4. Richard Stengel. *Information Wars: How We Lost the Global Battle Against Disinformation & What We Can Do About It*. New York: Atlantic Monthly Press, 2019, p. 292.

CHAPTER THREE: CLICKBAIT AND FAKE PHOTOS

5. Quoted in Bryan Gardiner, "You'll Be Outraged at How Easy It Was to Get You to Click on This Headline," *Wired*, December 18, 2015. www.wired.com.

6. Quoted in Mark Landler and Lauren Leatherby, "Princess of Wales Apologizes, Saying She Edited Image," *New York Times*, March 14, 2024. www.nytimes.com.

CHAPTER FOUR: SPOTTING FALSE INFORMATION

7. "SciCheck," *FactCheck.org,* n.d. www.factcheck.org/scicheck.

8. Xavier Harding, "Misinfo Monday: How to Spot Misinformation Like the Pros," *Mozilla*, August 3, 2020. http://foundation.mozilla.org.

FOR FURTHER RESEARCH

BOOKS

Robin Terry Brown, *Breaking the News.* Washington, DC:
National Geographic Kids, 2020.

Joyce Grant, *Can You Believe It?: How to Spot Fake News and Find the Facts*. Toronto, ON: Kids Can Press, 2022.

Heather C. Hudak, *How to Evaluate Sources of Information.*
San Diego, CA: BrightPoint Press, 2025.

INTERNET SOURCES

Xavier Harding, "Misinfo Monday: How to Spot Misinformation Like the Pros," *Mozilla*, August 3, 2020. http://foundation.mozilla.org.

"Misinformation and Disinformation: Thinking Critically about Information Sources," *College of Staten Island: CSI Library*, February 18, 2024. http://library.csi.cuny.edu.

"The Ultimate Guide to Propaganda," *Adobe Express*,
September 16, 2022. www.adobe.com.

WEBSITES

Associated Press: Not Real News
http://apnews.com/hub/not-real-news

AP's Not Real News page focuses on fake news stories and pieces of false information that have gone viral. The site is updated each week with information about fake photos, deepfake videos, and false news stories from different sources.

FactCheck.org
www.factcheck.org

FactCheck.org is one of the leading fact-checking sites. It tracks down false and misleading information on a wide range of topics. The site publishes detailed posts about these stories and their origins.

PolitiFact
www.politifact.com

PolitiFact is an award-winning, nonpartisan fact-checking website. The organization evaluates the validity of viral claims. Its website allows users to search for specific claims and to browse claims by politician or topic.

INDEX

ads, 15, 20, 26, 29, 36, 40
Associated Press, 41, 43–44

Berger, Jonah, 40–41

Captain America, 34
clickbait, 36, 38–41
confirmation bias, 20
conspiracy theories, 16, 17–19, 51
COVID-19 pandemic, 16, 19, 51

disinformation, 9, 11, 12, 35, 50

editors, 16, 43–44, 46, 50

Facebook, 28, 38–39
fact-checking, 16, 48, 50–53, 57
fake images, 41–47, 53–54
fake news, 9, 12, 15–17, 39, 41, 50, 54, 56

Harding, Xavier, 54
headlines, 6, 11, 15, 16, 28, 36–41

Kennedy, John F., 19, 51

Lee, Alfred, 26
Lee, Elizabeth, 26

Middleton, Kate, 42–44
misinformation, 9, 12, 54
moon landing, 17–19

New York Sun, 6, 8–9
North Korea, 31–33

Onion, The, 12, 14

Poe, Edgar Allan, 9
propaganda, 24, 26–35

reverse image search, 47

satire, 12–14
SIFT method, 23
social media, 15, 16, 20, 28, 44–45
Stengel, Richard, 35

TinEye, 47

Washington Post, 50

Zeidman-Karpinski, Annie, 23

IMAGE CREDITS

Cover: © Bongkarn Thanyakij/iStockphoto

5: © LumiNola/iStockphoto

7: © James D. McCabe/*Lights and Shadows of New York Life*

8: © Everett Collection/Shutterstock Images

10: © Tero Vesalainen/iStockphoto

13: © Feri Dhani Hasri/iStockphoto

14: © Valiantsin Suprunovich/Shutterstock Images

18: © NASA

21: © Vic Hinterlang/Shutterstock Images

22: © Eduard Figueres/iStockphoto

25: © Dennis MacDonald/Shutterstock Images

27: © Tero Vesalainen/Shutterstock Images

31: © Ground Picture/Shutterstock Images

32: © Attila Jandi/Shutterstock Images

34: © Nuamfolio/Shutterstock Images

37: © Prathankarnpap/Shutterstock Images

38: © Jeff Bukowski/Shutterstock Images

42: © Pete Hancock/Shutterstock Images

45: © Aiman Khair/Shutterstock Images

46: © Guillermo Spelucin Runciman/iStockphoto

49: © Tada Images/Shutterstock Images

52: © Michael Vi/Shutterstock Images

55: © svetikd/iStockphoto

57: © Iconic Space/Shutterstock Images

ABOUT THE AUTHOR

Tom Streissguth is the author of more than 150 books of history, biography, and media studies for young people. He is a graduate of Yale University, where he majored in music, and has worked as a teacher and book editor. His website *The Archive of American Journalism,* which collects nonfiction articles from more than a dozen renowned American writers, has become an important resource for students and authors.